W9-BKU-822

0 1021 0172820 6

Carol Dommermuth-Costa

Lerner Publications Company
Minneapolis

To LN for love, encouragement, and the gift of understanding during those times when the muse whispers to me and I can't turn away

According to scholars, only two authentic likenesses of William Shakespeare exist. In this book, they appear on pages 2 and 95.

A&E and **BIOGRAPHY** are trademarks of the A&E Television Networks, registered in the United States and other countries.

Some of the people profiled in this series have also been featured in A&E's acclaimed BIOGRAPHY series, which is available on videocassette from A&E Home Video. Call 1-800-423-1212 to order.

Lerner Publications Company
A division of Lerner Publishing Group
241 First Avenue North
Minneapolis, MN 55401 U.S.A.

Website address: www.lernerbooks.com

Library of Congress Cataloging-in-Publication Data

Dommermuth-Costa, Carol.
    William Shakespeare / by Carol Dommermuth-Costa.
       p.   cm. — (A&E biography)
    Includes bibliographical references and index.
    ISBN: 0-8225-4996-4 (lib. bdg. : alk. paper)
    1. Shakespeare, William, 1564–1616—Juvenile literature.
    2. Dramatists, English—Early modern, 1500–1700—Biography—Juvenile literature. [1. Shakespeare, William, 1564–1616. 2. Authors, English.] I. Title. II. Biography (Lerner Publications Company)
    PR2895.D53 2002
    822.3'3—dc21   00–011959

Manufactured in the United States of America
1 2 3 4 5 6 – JR – 07 06 05 04 03 02

CONTENTS

An artist's idea of what William Shakespeare might have looked like while at work in his study

EPIGRAPH

All the world's a stage,
And all the men and women merely players.
They have their exits and their entrances,
And one man in his time plays many parts,
His acts being seven ages. At first the infant,
Mewling and puking in the nurse's arms.
Then the whining schoolboy, with his satchel
And shining morning face, creeping like snail
Unwillingly to school. And then the lover,
Sighing like furnace, with a woeful ballad
Made to his mistress' eyebrow. Then a soldier,
Full of strange oaths and bearded like the pard,
Jealous in honour, sudden and quick in quarrel,
Seeking the bubble reputation
Even in the cannon's mouth. And then the justice,
In fair round belly with good capon lined,
With eyes severe and beard of formal cut,
Full of wise saws and modern instances,
And so he plays his part. The sixth age shifts
Into the lean and slipper'd Pantaloon,
With spectacles on nose and pouch on side,
His youthful hose, well saved, a world too wide
For his shrunk shank, and his big manly voice,
Turning again toward childish treble, pipes
And whistles in his sound. Last scene of all,
That ends this strange eventful history,
Is second childishness and mere oblivion,
Sans teeth, sans eyes, sans taste, sans everything.

— William Shakespeare, *As You Like It*, Act II, scene vii

7

London's theatergoers were entertained by many interesting characters such as the Simpleton, or fool, upper right.

INTRODUCTION

All the world's a stage,
And all the men and women merely players.
They have their exits and their entrances,
And one man in his time plays many parts,
His acts being seven ages.

One day during the summer of 1587, twenty-three-year-old William Shakespeare was standing outside the Theatre in London, England. Built in 1570, when Shakespeare was six years old, the Theatre was famous because it was London's first playhouse.

By 1570 theaters, or playhouses, had become so popular that London authorities regarded them as a public nuisance. Plays attracted great crowds of people, especially young men who neglected churchgoing for entertainment. The plays sometimes contained what was then considered foul language and raised controversial ideas about the government. Theaters also attracted pickpockets, fights, and the risk of spreading the plague, a deadly disease.

Shakespeare was waiting for the Theatre's patrons to arrive. It was customary for wealthy Londoners to travel to the theater on horseback or in fancy, horse-drawn carriages. Will Shakespeare was one of the young men hired to tend the horses while the patrons enjoyed the show. It wasn't the job Will had come to

This statue in Stratford-upon-Avon, England—Shakespeare's place of birth—pays tribute to the playwright.

London to seek, but it gave him a taste of theater life. He was hoping, eventually, to make the necessary connections to gain entrance to the inner sanctum, the stage. Months later, Shakespeare's idea paid off when he made the acquaintance of a troupe of actors called the Lord Chamberlain's Men. He became an actor, which changed his life forever. Will went on to become one of the greatest English-language poets and playwrights the world has ever known.

Stratford-upon-Avon is a popular tourist attraction. Stratford is about seventy-five miles northwest of London.

Chapter **ONE**

THE TOWN OF STRATFORD

At first the infant,
Mewling and puking in the nurse's arms.

STRATFORD-UPON-AVON, IN THE COUNTY OF WAR-
wickshire, England, was the birthplace and childhood
home of William Shakespeare. The River Avon runs
outside the town and at that time provided water for
its fifteen hundred inhabitants. The shop of the village
smithy, or blacksmith, was located near the market on
Chapel Lane, and the more affluent shopkeepers and
brewers lived at the bottom of High Street. The
apothecary, or pharmacist, also lived on this street
and sold licorice, aniseed, and some new items such
as tobacco and sassafras that had recently been im-
ported from America. The town had three inns—the

Swan, the Bear, and the Angel—that regularly hosted traveling troupes of actors. Houses with thatched roofs lined the streets, and children could usually be seen playing tag and other childhood games while their mothers chatted with neighbors. Merchants strolled through the town with their goods on their backs, singing their "peddling" songs.

Stratford had many laws. For instance, residents could be fined for letting their dogs go unmuzzled, for allowing a duck to wander onto a neighbor's property, for playing cards or any other games, for allowing their children to stay out past eight o'clock in the summertime, for not sweeping their gutters, or for borrowing gravel from the town gravel pits. The fines collected for breaking the law provided a generous source of revenue for the town politicians.

William Shakespeare was born in the family house on Stratford's Henley Street on or about April 23, 1564. Few birth records were kept in England at that time, but baptisms were recorded. An entry in the Stratford Parish baptismal register reads, "Guilemus filius Johannes Shakspere." The translation of this Latin record reads, "William son of John Shakspere," and it is dated April 26, 1564. In sixteenth-century England, most baptisms took place within a few days after the birth of a child, so scholars have set the date of April 23 for William Shakespeare's birth. William was the third of nine children born to Mary Arden and John Shakespeare but the first to live beyond infancy.

Shakespeare's mother, Mary Arden, owned this cottage, which still stands in Warwickshire, England.

Most of the information about Shakespeare's father is gleaned from town records, but there is a notable absence of information about Shakespeare's mother, Mary Arden. She was the eighth daughter of Agnes and Robert Arden, owners of Snitterfield Farm. Although Mary was a farmer's daughter, she was related to a family of social standing. Robert died in 1556, a year before Mary and John married. Mary's father left her a large legacy including money and land. Giving a woman this much responsibility was unheard of at that time in history, but apparently Shakespeare's mother was a capable woman who successfully handled her father's affairs. Scholars believe that her competency probably contributed to her husband's success in business.

John's father, Richard Shakespeare, was a tenant farmer on the Arden's property. Richard Shakespeare had expected his son to work as a farmer—as he had

Gloves were a popular fashion accessory in England during Shakespeare's time. These gloves belonged to Queen Elizabeth I and are decorated with gold embroidery.

done, but that profession was not to John's liking. Sometime in 1564, John became a merchant. He had many business interests and was an entrepreneur who seized many opportunities to make money. For example, almost everyone in the sixteenth century wore gloves, so John Shakespeare saw glove making as a profitable trade. Glovers were one of the most powerful trade groups in Stratford, and they were given the most strategic stalls in the Stratford market.

As a glover, John manufactured leather goods. He was also a "whitawer"—a dealer in fine white leather from which the best products were made. John also had a "woolshop" on Henley Street, where he sold wool and timber. He was also a moneylender and a wool merchant, two practices that got him into legal trouble because he was not licensed for those trades. John also sold barley to the local ale- and beer-brewing industry. He spent some time traveling to sell his wares at markets outside of Stratford, and young Will probably went with his father on many of his journeys.

John Shakespeare made one of his first appearances in the town records when he and two of his neighbors were each fined twelve pence (about twenty dollars in modern money). They were fined for establishing a garbage dump near their houses instead of using the official public dump at the end of the street.

In 1570 John Shakespeare was accused of breaking usury laws by charging interest on loans he made to neighbors, which was illegal at the time. Yet John Shakespeare's minor criminal offenses did not prevent him from holding political office. In 1560 he had been appointed an ale taster. He made sure the brewers of beer or ale were putting "no hops nor no other subtle things in their brewing," and that the women who sold the beer weren't serving it in unsealed pots. The next year, John entered the council, the governing body of Stratford. At one time, he served as a constable, responsible for breaking up petty fights and quarrels.

CURRENCY VALUES

Each country has its own basic units of money. The value of one nation's money expressed in another nation's money is called the exchange rate. Exchange rates vary from day to day, and they are based on many factors. The chart below shows currency in Shakespeare's time at the left, with modern dollar equivalents to the right.

ENGLISH MONEY	U.S. DOLLAR (APPROXIMATE)
1 pound = 20 shillings	$400.00
1 shilling = 12 pence	$20.00
1 penny	$1.66

Gold Coins

1 sovereign = 1 pound	$400.00
1 royal = 10–14 shillings	$200.00–280.00
1 angel = 7–10 shillings	$140.00–200.00

Silver Coins

1 crown = 5 shillings	$100.00
4 crowns = 1 pound	$400.00
1 half-crown = 2½ shillings	$50.00
1 sixpence = half a shilling	$10.00
1 groat = 4 pence	$6.60
1 threepenny piece = 3 pence	$5.00
1 threefarthing piece = ¾ penny	$1.20
1 halfpenny piece	$.80

Then he was made petty constable. John went on to hold several other offices during his lifetime, including that of alderman and "balyf" (mayor) of Stratford.

When John left the farm to become an independent tradesman, he served a seven-year apprenticeship to become a member of the Craft of Glovers, Whitawers, and Collarmakers. Stratford records show that he was already selling gloves in Henley Street in 1552. John and Mary owned their own house and shop in the bustling town of Stratford, and the future looked bright for the young couple.

Little is known about William Shakespeare's childhood years, but his exposure to theater is likely to have begun at an early age. In 1569 a traveling troupe of actors called the Queen's Men came to Stratford to perform at the Swan Inn. The next spring, Stratford citizens welcomed another troupe called the Earl of Worcester's Men. They performed in the courtyard at the Angel Inn to a rousing crowd. Because John liked theater, he probably took Will to see these troupes.

In London, as in other towns, actors used the open, rectangular courtyards of the local inns as theaters. Actors worked on a scaffold at one end of the courtyard, and the audience gathered around them. The wealthier members of the audience used the seats in some of the upstairs rooms of the inns to peer down on the production.

This arrangement had its drawbacks. First, the actors had to share the use of the yard with the carters,

This 1876 wood carving shows a play being performed in the courtyard of a London inn.

who carried the freight and mail to and from London on certain days of the week. Consequently, the actors could only use the courtyards on three days of the week. It was also difficult to collect money for admission, and there was no private place to change costumes. These concerns were considered unimportant to most of the actors, however. As long as they had an audience, they were happy performing.

As a youngster, Will may have been seated on his father's shoulders. Watching as the players frolicked and cantered in their colorful costumes and handmade props, Will may have marveled at the bold manner in which the actors spoke their lines and played their different roles. Young Will may have envied the actors and thought that when he was old enough, he would pursue his dream of joining them. But first the young man had to obtain a good education.

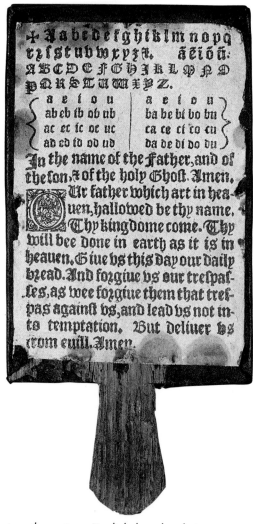

This seventeenth century English hornbook (a one-page book for beginning readers) is like the one Shakespeare would have used when learning to read a century earlier.

Chapter **TWO**

SCHOOLBOY

Then the whining schoolboy, with his satchel
And shining morning face, creeping like snail
Unwillingly to school.

WILL **SHAKESPEARE PROBABLY BEGAN HIS EDUCA-**
tion by entering a petty school when he was about
seven years old. Children learned basic reading and
writing at home before entering petty school. By modern standards, there wasn't much to read, and no
spelling standards existed. In the petty school, Will
learned numbers and simple calculations.

The purpose of petty school was to prepare students
for grammar school (grade school), and the main purpose of the grammar school was to teach Latin grammar, poetry, drama, and history. Knowledge of Latin

Tourists can still visit the grammar school that Shakespeare attended in Stratford-upon-Avon.

was necessary for many careers and was a sign of an educated person.

The grammar school in Stratford was called the King's New School of Stratford-upon-Avon. The school was designed to educate the children of public officials, so the standards were higher than those at most English grammar schools.

Will's teachers were university men with a fair amount of learning. Simon Hunt was master when Will began his schooling. Hunt, a graduate of Oxford University, was a fine teacher. Thomas Jenkins became schoolmaster in 1575, when Will was eleven. At that time, students had to follow strict rules, and teachers physically punished students who broke them. It is fairly certain, however, that Will did not experience abuse, because Master Hunt was a fair disciplinarian who believed that children respond more to love than to beatings.

Will began every morning with a lesson in classical Latin (the language of ancient Rome) and a review of the previous day's homework. He read and translated various authors such as Aesop (the author of *Fables*), Caesar, Virgil, and Ovid (Shakespeare's favorite). William also read Horace, Livy, and several Roman playwrights, such as Seneca and Plautus, the most admired writer of Latin comedy. William would also have read Cicero as well as studied ancient history and philosophy and a smattering of Greek. English was not taught in school during Shakespeare's time.

Scholars are able to make educated guesses about Shakespeare's reading material by noting the classical authors to whom he alludes in his plays. For instance, scholars assume that Shakespeare began his Latin studies with one of the well-known books of the time, the *Accidence*. Evidence of this comes from his play *The Merry Wives of Windsor*, which contains a dialogue that is quoted almost word-for-word from the *Accidence*. Shakespeare almost certainly studied John Lyly's *Grammaticus Latina*, the accepted textbook of the day.

Ovid, the ancient Roman poet who wrote The Metamorphoses, *was one of Shakespeare's favorite authors.*

The school day ended with a religious reading, the singing of hymns, and a prayer. Will and his friends left school around six o'clock in the evening. Young Will attended school about nine hours a day, six days a week, and he attended classes all year except for three short holiday periods.

Shakespeare's other source of education came from the Church of England. Homilies, or sermons, were a major part of religious education. It was mandatory that townspeople attend church on Sunday. Here preachers read passages from the Geneva Bible or the Bishop's Bible, *The Book of Common Prayer,* and *Acts and Monuments.*

Will Shakespeare probably attended school and played with other boys of his social class. Girls did not attend school at that time. Richard Quiney, who was several years older than Shakespeare, became one of Will's closest friends. Richard wrote the only surviving letter to Shakespeare. His intimate form of address indicates the respect he had for his friend. He begins, *"My loving and good friend and countryman Wm. Shakespeare."* Thomas Greene was another of Shakespeare's friends. In his diary, Greene refers to Will as "my cosen [cousin] Shakespeare." Other playmates in William's group included William Smith, George Cawdrey, and Richard Field, who lived on Bridge Street near the Shakespeares' house.

When William and his friends were allowed to play—during their schoolroom breaks, after church services on Sundays, and during holidays—they enjoyed a variety of games. Hide-and-seek was a popular game and was called by different names, such as "hoop-and-hide" and "harry-racket." Blindman's bluff, sometimes called "the hoodwinke play" or "hoodman-blinde," and tag were other games William and his friends enjoyed.

There are no records that show how long William Shakespeare remained at grammar school. But his first biographer, Nicholas Rowe, indicates that the need of his assistance at home forced his father to withdraw him from school. In fact, John Shakespeare was going through some difficult times around 1577. Although there are no records of debts, his finances were quickly being depleted. He also failed on several occasions to attend the mandatory meetings for all public officers at the Guild Hall and was fined accordingly. Scholars speculate that John Shakespeare's absence may have been due to depression or embarrassment over his financial problems. Whatever the reasons, young Will's

Sixteenth-century Flemish painter Pieter Brueghel the Elder portrayed many detailed scenes of everyday life. Above is his painting Children's Games, *which shows "hoop-and-hide" and other games of Shakespeare's time.*

father probably asked him to help with the family business. At the age of thirteen, Will's school days ended forever. Two years later, Will's sister Anne—not quite eight years old—died. His brother Edmund was born the following year, in May 1580. By then Will was sixteen, his brother Gilbert was fourteen, his sister Joan was eleven, and his brother Richard was six.

The Handfast *depicts the betrothal of William Shakespeare and Anne Hathaway in 1582. The couple is shown in the background.*

Chapter **THREE**

BETROTHED AND WED

And then the lover,
Sighing like furnace, with a woeful ballad
Made to his mistress' eyebrow.

NOT MUCH IS KNOWN ABOUT THE CIRCUMSTANCES OF Shakespeare's life from the time he left school until about the age of eighteen. Some scholars speculate that Will worked with his father in business. Some think he worked in the legal profession. This latter theory is based on the fact that Shakespeare demonstrates a prolific knowledge of legal terms in his plays. However, experts know that around 1581 Will began a romantic relationship with Anne Hathaway.

Anne was born in 1556 to Richard and Joan Hathaway. The Shakespeares counted the Hathaways among their long-time friends, and in 1566 John Shakespeare even paid Richard Hathaway's debts.

The only image of Anne Hathaway is a faded drawing in a copy of Shakespeare's *Third Folio*. In this sketch, Anne Hathaway is shown to be a large woman with a high forehead. Shakespeare biographer Russell Fraser describes the woman in the drawing: "The eyebrows are severely plucked, the nose strong and fleshy. Expressionless but wide-awake, the eyes show nothing behind them. The lips, sensuous, are compressed, the chin heavy and decisive."

The Hathaways owned Hewlands Farm in the village of Shottery. The farm stood at the edge of the Forest of Arden and was about one mile west of Stratford. It was within easy walking distance for Will, and he had had ample opportunity to visit the Hathaways over the years.

Historians are not sure how long Will courted Anne before they were married—or whether they were married at all. Records in the nearby town of Worcester show that on November 28, 1582, Anne Hathaway, who was twenty-six years old, and William Shakespeare, who was eighteen years old, applied for and received their marriage license. The marriage bond stated that "willm Shagspere on th one ptie [party], and Anne hethwey of Stratfor in the Dioces of Worcester maiden may lawfully solennize mariony [matrimony] together and in the same afterward remaine and contew [continue] like man and wiffe [wife]."

ANNE HATHAWAY'S HOUSE?

n Shakespeare's play *As You Like It*, Oliver asks Celia where he can find "a sheepcote fenced about with olive trees." Some scholars believe that Celia's response is an accurate description of Anne Hathaway's house, *below*.

West of this place, down in the neighbour bottom.
The rank of osiers by the murmuring stream
Left on your right hand brings you to the place.
But at this hour the house doth keep itself,
There's none within.

—As You Like It, Act IV, scene iii

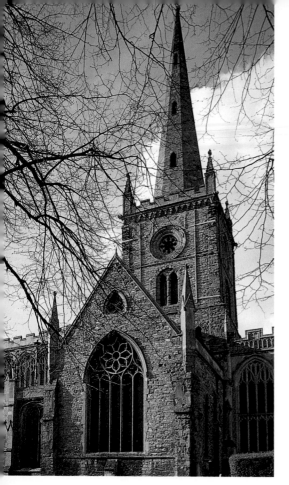

Stratford-upon-Avon's Holy Trinity Church is probably where the wedding banns of William Shakespeare and Anne Hathaway were announced.

Marriage certificates did not exist in the sixteenth century. When two people wanted to marry, it was common practice to first ask the church's pastor to read the banns, or announce the couple's intention to marry, on three successive Sundays. Reading the banns gave the community ample time to dispute the marriage if there was just cause. For instance, if a person engaged to marry one person was already married to someone else, was related to the betrothed, or was already engaged to another, church members were obliged to make the situation known to the pastor. If, after three readings of the banns, no one in the village came forward to dispute the marriage, the wedding usually took place several months later.

But Anne and Will's betrothal was unusual because Anne was three months pregnant. In this situation, haste was important, so William had to apply to the Ordinary, or lawyer, of the village for a dispensation, or exception, to the usual arrangement. The dispensation was granted, and the banns were read only once instead of the usual three times.

Since Will was under the age of twenty-one, he needed the permission of his parents to marry. Then Will had to swear that he had not been married before, that he was not related to Anne, and that he was not engaged to any other woman. He was reminded that if he lied and it was later discovered that he had not told the truth, he would be fined 40 pounds (about sixteen thousand dollars), a good sum of money at that time. Two friends of the Hathaways witnessed Will taking this oath.

No records exist proving that the couple were officially married in Holy Trinity Church or in any other nearby church. However, it was not uncommon in the sixteenth century for couples to be considered husband and wife after they had received their marriage license, had the banns read, and lived together for a number of years. The actual ceremony was not a legal necessity. Some scholars suggest that this may have been the case with Will and Anne.

A HOUSEWIFE'S CHORES

T his excerpt from *Women in England c. 1275–1525* explains the typical chores of an English housewife during Shakespeare's time.

". . . and when you are up and ready, then first sweep the house, set the table, and put everything in your house in order. Milk your cows, suckle your calves, strain your milk, get your children up and dress them, and provide for your husband's breakfast, dinner, supper, and for your children and servants, and take your place with them. Send corn and malt to the mill so that you can bake and brew whenever there is need. . . .

You must make butter and cheese whenever you are able,

feed your pigs both morning and evening, and give your poultry their food in the morning. . . .

It is a wife's occupation to winnow all kinds of grain, to make malt, to wash and wring, to make hay, reap corn, and in time of need to help her husband fill the muck-wain or dung cart, drive the plough, load hay, corn, and such other, and to go or ride to the market, sell butter, cheese, milk, eggs, chickens, capons, hens, pigs, geese, and all types of grain, and also to buy all sorts of things necessary for the household, and to make a true reckoning and account to her husband of what she has spent."

Other scholars question whether William Shakespeare was originally engaged to another woman. In addition to the November 28, 1582, application for a marriage license, records dated the day before—November 27, 1582—state that a marriage license was sought "inter [between] willelmum Shaxperre et Annam whateley [Anne Whateley] de Temple grafton [of Temple Grafton]." Had Will actually intended to marry Anne Whateley instead of Anne Hathaway? When the Hathaway family discovered Anne was pregnant, did they force Will to marry her? Did the record reflect a writing error? Or, since Shakespeare

Anne and William Shakespeare moved into the Shakespeare family's house on Henley Street shortly after their marriage.

was a common name at the time, did the November 27 entry refer to another couple? We will probably never know for sure.

After their marriage, Will and Anne moved into the Shakespeare house on Henley Street. Six months later, Susanna was born. She was christened on Sunday, May 26, 1583. Two years later, in 1585, Anne gave

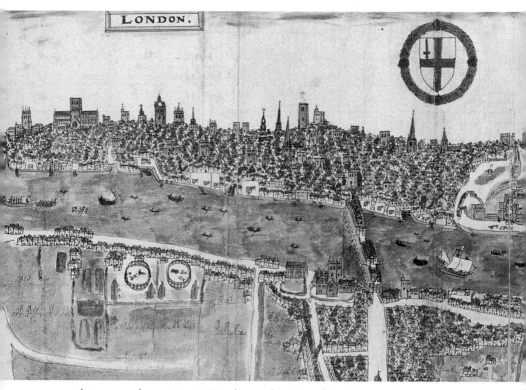

This map, drawn in 1588, shows the city of London on the banks of the River Thames.

birth to twins, Judith and Hamnet, named after close friends of the Shakespeare family.

Scholars aren't sure how Will supported his growing family. Some think he taught school or became a tutor. Some think he worked in the legal profession. He may have helped his father in the family shop. The last written record indicating that Shakespeare lived in Stratford dates to 1588, when he and his parents issued a legal complaint against his cousin Lambert. After that date, no records exist to indicate what William Shakespeare was doing or where he was living. Sometime during this period, however, Will made his way to London, leaving the family in Stratford. Scholars call this period "the lost years."

Mary Stuart, Queen of Scots, was found guilty of plotting to kill Queen Elizabeth I. Mary was beheaded in 1587.

Chapter **FOUR**

THE LOST YEARS

Then a soldier,
Full of strange oaths and bearded like the pard,
Jealous in honour, sudden and quick in quarrel,
Seeking the bubble reputation
Even in the cannon's mouth.

HISTORICALLY, THERE WAS A GREAT DEAL GOING ON in Shakespeare's part of the world during the period of his life that scholars refer to as "the lost years." In 1586 Mary Stuart, Queen of Scots had been tried for treason in her plot to kill Queen Elizabeth I. She was executed in 1587 in front of spectators who had come out to see the beheading. In 1588 the Spanish king, Philip II, sent his invincible armada, consisting of 130 armored ships carrying 27,000 men, to

This English engraving depicts the defeat of the Spanish Armada in 1588.

invade England. The war raged for weeks, but the English fleet was victorious. It defeated the armada, destroying more than half the ships after a major storm in the English Channel pushed many of the Spanish ships off course and into the arms of the English.

That same storm was responsible for a terrible flood in Shakespeare's hometown of Stratford-upon-Avon. The flood made an indelible imprint in the memory of its inhabitants. The floodwater destroyed Clopton's Bridge, a landmark in the town.

In the literary world, Christopher Marlowe published *Dr. Faustus* in 1589. This tragic drama depicts the struggle of a university man who sells his soul to the devil. This was followed by another famous work, *The Jew of Malta,* in 1590.

There are no written accounts of William Shakespeare's activities in London between 1587 and 1591. Scholars generally agree that he entered the theater as an actor and playwright during this period. By the time Shakespeare burst into the limelight in 1592, he was already well known in the theater world.

The first written reference to Shakespeare in London appeared in Robert Greene's pamphlet, *Greene's Groatsworth of Wit, Bought with a Million of Repentance Describing the Folly of Youth, the Falsehood of Makeshift Flatterers, the Misery of the Negligent, and Mischiefs of Deceiving Courtesans.* Robert Greene was a novelist and playwright who was angry and bitter over the rise to prominence of younger writers such as Christopher Marlowe, Thomas Nashe, Thomas Kyd, and William Shakespeare. Greene lambasted these fresh, new playwrights and denounced their talent. In his *Groatsworth of Wit,* Greene recalled the mistakes of his youth and described the bitterness he felt toward the fresh, young actors and writers who profited, he believed, from his writing. Greene, after all, had a bachelor's degree from Cambridge. The others did not have university degrees. Greene believed that actors were gaining fame and fortune from words he—a writer and scholar—had written. He also felt some, such as Shakespeare, were even trying to surpass Greene by writing their own plays.

Greene's work, published after his death in 1592, was written sometime between 1587 and the date of publication. In *Groatsworth of Wit*, Greene refers to William Shakespeare as "an upstart crow, beautified with our feathers, that with his Tygers hart wrapt in a player's hyde, [tiger's heart wrapped in a player's hide, or skin] supposes he is well able to bombast out a blanke verse as the best of you: and beeing an absolute Johannes fac totum [Jack of all trades], is in his owne conceit the only Shake-scene in a country."

The term *Shake-scene* is a clear reference to William Shakespeare and is the first evidence of his fame in the London theater. Shakespeare must have been well known as a playwright for Greene to mention him by name. Greene refers to Shakespeare as a jack of all trades, or a man who could do many things but none of them well. Shakespeare must have demonstrated several talents—including that of a gifted poet. Finally, Greene's parody of a line from Shakespeare's *Henry VI*, Part III— "O Tygers hart wrapt in a woman's hyde,"—indicates that Shakespeare's play had become so popular by then that lines from the play had become familiar reference points.

Much of what is known about Shakespeare's life comes from secondary sources—people other than Shakespeare, such as Greene—writing about the playwright's life. Even the dates of Shakespeare's plays and poetry—from which scholars can construct a chronology of his life—are difficult to determine. No one knows exactly when the various plays were written, in part because dates were not given much importance at the time. In addition, Shakespeare's plays were not published until 1623, seven years after his death, and no original manuscripts survive.

Scholars speculate that after Shakespeare wrote a play, he hired a scribe to make copies for the actors so they could learn their lines. These copies, called "foul papers," often contained stage directions and comments by the author. Copying the play was long and tiring work, and copies were often full of small errors. Sometimes by the time the play arrived at the printer, it had been somewhat changed. Also, the work underwent another change in the process of printing. To facilitate the setting of type, the printer often had his assistant read the work to him while he placed the letters by hand. This practice led to errors in reading, hearing, and setting the final version.

Writers in Shakespeare's time were also threatened with the possibility that someone else could lay claim to their work. Modern copyright law, which protects writers and artists from anyone stealing their work, didn't exist. The only protection writers of the era had was the printer recording the work in a book called *The Stationers' Register*, which showed the date, the author's name, and the title of the work. But in the

Printing was faster than having scribes copy a work by hand, but it was still a slow process.

case of plays, the manuscripts belonged to the acting company, which retained them until the play lost its popularity. Then they were discarded. It is a wonder that so many of Shakespeare's plays survived.

Despite these difficulties, scholars can approximate the dates of some of his plays from other written records. For example, Greene referred to *Henry VI*, Part I and *Henry VI*, Part III. These plays were probably written between 1587 (when Shakespeare moved to London) and 1592 (when the works by Greene were published).

In 1592 an epidemic of plague erupted in London. The city had more sick and dead than any other city in England. Officials told people to move to isolated areas and to stay away from crowds. Local authorities forbade all gatherings—except church services—within a seven-mile radius of the city. All the theaters closed.

Many people believed theater was immoral and against God's law. They felt that, through the plague, God was punishing humanity for acting in and attending the theater. They wanted to close the theaters permanently. But there were more Londoners—including the queen—who enjoyed the theater than there were religious zealots. The theaters reopened after the plague ended—almost two years later.

Londoners fled the city to escape the deadly plague, which periodically erupted in England.

THE BLACK DEATH

During Shakespeare's life, many people believed that the plague was carried in the air. People were desperate to try any and all remedies to avoid becoming sick from the plague. They burned incense made from juniper, lemon, camphor, and sulfur in their homes. When going outside, people placed handkerchiefs dipped in oils over their faces. Parsons, or clergymen, even rang the church bells incessantly to drive the plague from the town.

In fact, the bacillus organism is host to the plague. The organism is usually carried by fleas that infest animals such as rats and squirrels. The flea bites the animal, then transfers the blood of the animal into a human host when it bites a person. The infected animals and humans die, but oddly enough, the flea survives. Plague symptoms include high fever, aching limbs, and spitting up blood. The lymph nodes under the neck and armpits begin to swell and turn black. For this reason, the plague was known as the Black Death.

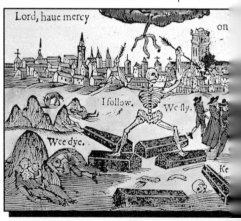

During the plague years when the theaters were closed, many actors and writers either died or had to give up their careers because they had no way to support themselves. Without the patronage (financial support) of the earl of Southhampton, Shakespeare might have been one of these lost talents. It is not clear whether Shakespeare returned to Stratford-upon-Avon during this time. No documentation exists to indicate that he did. Some scholars think Shakespeare used this time to devote himself to a new genre, the writing of sonnets.

When modern readers think of William Shakespeare, they think of him first as a playwright, then as an actor, and lastly as a poet. However, when 1593 came to a close, Shakespeare was known mostly for his poetry. The poems were his first publications and the first of his writings to appear with his name on the title page. (His name didn't appear on his plays until quite some time after he began producing them on the stage.)

Shakespeare's narrative poem *Venus and Adonis* is about a doomed romance between two beautiful but inexperienced lovers. It was published in April 1593 by his Stratford friend Richard Field—who had become a London printer. *Venus and Adonis* became so popular that ten editions were printed during Shakespeare's lifetime. To write the poem, Shakespeare borrowed ideas from Ovid's *Metamorphoses*.

Shakespeare's poem begins with a dedication to

Henry Wriothesley, third earl of Southampton and Baron of Titchfield, who was Shakespeare's patron (a wealthy person who helped support writers and artists). Shakespeare also dedicated his second narrative poem, *The Rape of Lucrece*, to the earl of Southampton. It is believed that Southampton gave Shakespeare the generous sum of one thousand pounds (about four hundred thousand U.S. dollars) for these two poems.

William Shakespeare's patron—Henry Wriothesley, third earl of Southhampton

Shakespeare also began writing sonnets at this time. The concept of a sonnet, which is a fourteen-line lyric poem, was devised and perfected by the fourteenth-century Italian poet Petrarch. Petrarch had established love of a woman as the theme of traditional sonnets. He wrote his sonnets in two units—the first in eight lines, the second in six lines. He also established a predetermined rhyming pattern.

Shakespeare broke with tradition when he wrote his first eighteen sonnets. He wrote his poems in three units of four lines each, with a concluding couplet (a two-line unit). The rhyming pattern in Shakespeare's sonnets also differs from Petrarch's rhyme scheme. And the theme of Shakespeare's sonnets is new. Such phrases as "thy sweet self" and "Shall I compare thee to a summer's day" are addressed to a young man, not to a young woman. Renaissance people admired beautiful young men as well as young women. Renaissance artists painted them and wrote about them. (The Renaissance was a great cultural movement in Europe that began in Italy in the 1300s and lasted into the 1600s.) In his sonnets, Shakespeare is acknowledging the attractive appearance of a young nobleman and suggesting that he marry so his beauty can be passed on to future generations. Also, Shakespeare had a duty to address this theme since he was writing under the patronage of the earl of Southhampton. Author A. L. Rowse points out that Southampton offered Shakespeare entry into a cultivated, wealthy, sophisticated society, opening up new contacts and experiences. Shakespeare had good reason to be grateful and to reflect his gratitude and sense of duty to his patron in sonnets of praise and honor.

In Shakespeare's first sonnet, the author reminds the young man of what he has to offer the world. He tells him not to be selfish with his talents.

> From fairest creatures we desire increase,
> That thereby beauty's rose might never die, . . .
> Thou that art now the world's fresh ornament
> And only herald to the gaudy [dazzling] spring,
> Within thine own bud bureiest thy content [your
>   child that might be]
> And, tender churl [miser], makest waste in
> niggarding [being selfish with your talents].

In the second sonnet, Shakespeare reminds the young man of the inevitability of aging. He tells him how wonderful it would be to know that he had passed on his beauty to his offspring.

> When forty winters shall besiege thy brow
> And dig deep trenches in thy beauty's field,
> Thy youth's proud livery [clothing], so gazed on
>   now,
> Will be a tatter'd weed [ragged garment], of small
>   worth held.
> Then being ask'd where all thy beauty lies,

Where all the treasure of thy lusty days, . . .
How much more praise deserved thy beauty's use
If thou couldst answer, "This fair child of mine
Shall sum my count [balance my account] and
make my old excuse [excuse for being old],"
Proving his beauty by succession [right of-
succession as your child] thine! . . .

In the late 1500s, many English authors wrote sonnets that followed a narrative pattern that was often autobiographical. For that reason, scholars have examined Shakespeare's sonnets to learn more about his life. They have not reached any agreement about the information contained in the sonnets. However, Shakespeare's sonnets do provide insight into the personality of the playwright. He was a sensitive man, open to emotions and feelings. He was capable of deep devotion, and when wronged, he learned to forgive.

Unlike Shakespeare's poems, his plays did not have many original plots. Shakespeare used Raphael Holinshed's *The Chronicles of England, Scotland, and Ireland*, first published in 1578, as a source for the tragedies *Macbeth* and *King Lear* and for most of his history plays.

Shakespeare adapted other plays from the Greek and Roman stories he read during his classical education. The plot for *The Comedy of Errors*, for example, was based on *The Menaechmi* by the ancient Roman playwright Plautus. The original play deals with identical

SHAKESPEARE'S WORKS (FROM ABOUT 1587 TO 1594)

History plays: *Henry IV, Richard II, Richard III, King John*

Comedies: *The Comedy of Errors, The Taming of the Shrew, The Two Gentlemen of Verona, Love's Labor's Lost, A Midsummer Night's Dream, The Merchant of Venice*

Tragedies: *Titus Andronicus, Romeo and Juliet*

A moral narrative poem: *The Rape of Lucrece*

An erotic narrative poem: *Venus and Adonis*

twins who cannot be told apart. Shakespeare gives his twins (both named Antipholus) servants who are also identical twins and both named Dromio. Both sets of twins are separated as children. When the brothers end up in the same city, a series of comical mix-ups occurs before the brothers are reunited. The play is a mixture of comedy and romance, and, like many of his plays, begins with sorrow but ends joyfully.

The plot for *All's Well That Ends Well* is taken from the Italian poet Boccaccio's *Decameron Tales*. In Shakespeare's play, Helena makes a pact with the King of France: if she cures his malady (illness), he will give her permission to marry Bertram, a nobleman whom she loves. Helena cures the king and marries Bertram. But Bertram considers Helena beneath him and deserts her after the wedding. Yet in the end, Bertram realizes his wife's good qualities and promises to love her. Many modern readers do not like the leading characters, but the play's interest lies in Shakespeare's effort to express his view of humanity's imperfections through the use of comedy.

When the theaters finally opened again after the plague epidemic, Shakespeare was one of the 114,000 Londoners who had survived the dread disease. He was well respected in the theater world, and he had enough money to enable him to live a comfortable life.

Shakespeare, on his knees at left, *was a gifted playwright and also a popular actor.*

Chapter FIVE

THE LORD CHAMBERLAIN'S MEN

And then the justice,
In fair round belly with good capon lined,
With eyes severe and beard of formal cut,
Full of wise saws and modern instances,
And so he plays his part.

MIDSUMMER NIGHT'S DREAM, A COMIC SATIRE, may have been written for a particular noble person's wedding, but experts don't know this for sure. The play is set in Athens, Greece, and revolves around the misunderstandings that take place in the relationships among three couples and in their relationships with other characters. The play soon became a great favorite in playhouses around London. It led to the establishment of a new group of actors called the Lord Chamberlain's Company or the Lord Chamberlain's Men. Shakespeare was a member of this troupe.

Most acting companies in Shakespeare's era took their names from an important person of the royal court who helped to support them. This practice of drawing court members to the theaters also protected actors from local authorities—who sometimes tried to close down the playhouses. The troupe's namesake also brought parties of people to the theater, which insured a lively audience. Lord Chamberlain was Henry Carey, first lord Hunsdon. (Almost every royal English court had chamberlains. They were high-ranking members of the court and advisers to the king or queen.)

The leading members of the Lord Chamberlain's Men were Richard and Cuthbert Burbage (sons of James Burbage, the actor who built the Theatre), William Kemp (a comedian), and Will Shakespeare (actor and playwright). The acting company was extremely successful, but it had stiff competition from another acting company called the Admiral's Men. In 1594 the Lord Chamberlain's Men presented two of Shakespeare's plays, A *Midsummer Night's Dream* and *Love's Labor's Lost*, at Queen Elizabeth's court. Both productions received an enthusiastic response.

With its newly won success, the acting company played not only in public playhouses and at court but also toured and played at various inns in and around London. By the end of 1594, Shakespeare had written

Richard Burbage became a well-known actor because of his talented performances in tragedies.

Henry VI (all three parts), *Richard III, Titus Andronicus, The Two Gentlemen of Verona, The Taming of the Shrew, The Comedy of Errors,* and *Love's Labor's Lost.*

By August 1596, thirty-two-year-old William Shakespeare had become a prosperous, established writer. His career as both actor and author was a major success. His popular plays were being performed, and his poems were selling well. Shakespeare thought of going into semiretirement. By modern standards, a man in his thirties is still considered young. In the sixteenth century, however, when most people did not live past the age of fifty-five, a man of Shakespeare's age was perceived as well past his prime. As Shakespeare was pondering his future, tragedy struck. His eleven-year-old son, Hamnet, died.

The circumstances of Hamnet's death are unknown, but Shakespeare must have felt enormous grief. At least one scholar thinks that Shakespeare expressed

the pain of losing a child in his play *King John*. In
Act III, Constance is grief stricken over the death of
her child, Arthur, Duke of Bretagne and nephew of
King John.

> Grief fills the room up of my absent child,
> Lies in his bed, walks up and down with me,
> Puts on his pretty looks, repeats his words,
> Remembers me of all his gracious parts,
> Stuffs out his vacant garments with his form;
> Then have I reason to be fond of Grief.
> Fare you well. Had you such loss as I,
> I could give better comfort than you do.
> I will not keep this form upon my head
> When there is such disorder in my wit.
> O Lord! My boy, my Arthur, my fair son!
> My life, my joy, my food, my all the world!
> My widow-comfort, and my sorrows' cure!

—*King John*, Act III, scene iv, 93–98

The next spring, in 1597, Shakespeare decided to re-
turn home to Stratford-upon-Avon. Reunited with his
wife and daughters, he purchased New Place (on the
corner of Chapel Street and Chapel Lane), the second
largest house in town.

The house, with three stories and five gables, had a
small front court built by Sir Hugh Clopton in the latter part of the fifteenth century. The property had two

barns, two greenhouses, and several small gardens that ran down to the river. The house was large and roomy, with fireplaces in almost every room. Shakespeare lost no time settling Anne and his two daughters, fourteen-year-old Susanna and twelve-year-old Judith, into the house. While his family enjoyed their new home, Shakespeare went back to work writing more plays. He completed *The Merchant of Venice, The Merry Wives of Windsor,* and *Much Ado about Nothing.*

At the end of 1598, Shakespeare returned to London and found that his acting company had no place to perform. The landowner, Giles Allen, refused to renew the lease. Allen even laid claim to the bricks and timbers James Burbage had used to build the Theatre.

Frustrated and without a playhouse, the Chamberlain's Men decided to build another theater. In December 1598, they found a plot of land across the River Thames in Southwark and secured a thirty-one-year lease. Seven of the Chamberlain's Men, including Shakespeare, bought shares in the theater. They would never again be homeless.

The Chamberlain's Men performed for Queen Elizabeth on Christmas Day. Three days later, six actors from the Chamberlain's Men, a group of workmen, and a master carpenter stormed the Theatre. They removed most of the bricks and timbers and ferried them across the river to Southwark, the site for their new playhouse.

Elizabeth I was queen during much of Shakespeare's life. Her hand rests on a globe, left, *symbolizing her role in making England a world power.*

Work on the theater, which would hold an audience of three thousand people, began almost immediately. The troupe chose a name for their new playhouse—the Globe—that reflected their belief that "all the world's a stage," a phrase later used in Act II of Shakespeare's *As You Like It.*

The design of the Globe was similar to James
Burbage's Theatre but included certain additions.
Shakespeare and his troupe knew from experience
what amenities they wanted in a theater. They laid out
plans for the builder to include wardrobe rooms, pul-
leys in the roof, and trapdoors for setting up and re-
moving props. Actors entered and left the stage
through two doors at the back of the stage. Behind
the doors were tiring (dressing) rooms. A silk flag flew
from a turret on the roof when the play was ready to
be performed. A trumpeter sounded the signal for the
townspeople to rush to the theater. The third trumpet
blow meant that the play was starting.

No curtain hid the stage. The stage jutted out and
was surrounded on three sides by the audience. They

*The Globe stage was built,
like most English theaters of
the time, so the stage jutted
out and could be seen by
the audience on all three
sides.*

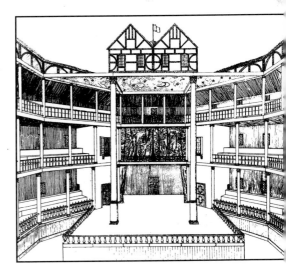

stood or sat on benches to watch the play. The audience had no playbills, no explanations of what the play was about, who the characters were, or where the play was set. Such information was learned from lines spoken between the characters. Or it was learned from asides, when the characters were thinking out loud and revealing plans to the audience. Communication between the actors and their audience was direct.

Julius Caesar *became one of Shakespeare's most popular history plays. Here a modern theater company performs the play at the Stratford Festival in Stratford, Ontario.*

No Women Onstage

Women were forbidden to act on the English stage. Acting companies used young boys, whose voices had not yet changed, to play the parts of women. The boys often had no choice in the matter and were sometimes "sold" to the acting company by families who needed money.

These boys were professionally coached by the senior members of the acting company and often became excellent actors and singers. Many of them continued their acting careers well into their adult years. This practice of using male children as actors was a serious bone of contention with the religious factions in London, who considered it scandalous that young boys would be forced to cross-dress as women.

One of the first plays performed in the new Globe was *Julius Caesar*. Shakespeare tried to have the play written for the opening of the Globe. He didn't make his deadline, but the play was performed soon afterward to a full house.

Julius Caesar, partly based on *The Lives of the Noble Grecians and Romans* by the ancient Greek biographer Plutarch, portrays the famous Roman general and his political battles and rivals. The play asks the question: What happens to a ruler whose appetite for power is never satisfied?

Although a reader would assume from the title of the play that Julius Caesar is the lead character, he is not. Brutus, a Roman general and Caesar's best friend, is the central character. Brutus thinks Caesar has overstepped his bounds and become a danger to Rome's best interests. Cassius is the plotter who convinces Brutus to kill Caesar for the good of the country. The plotters attack Caesar while he is in the Roman Senate. Brutus defends the act to a crowd of Roman citizens, but then lets Mark Antony, one of Caesar's loyal supporters, deliver an eloquent funeral speech. Standing over Caesar's body, Mark Antony declares, "Friends, Romans, countrymen, lend me your ears. I come to bury Caesar, not to praise him." He then goes on sarcastically to describe Brutus and the other plotters as "honourable men." He praises Caesar's virtues, shows his fatal wounds, and turns the crowd into an angry mob that wants to kill the plotters, who flee Rome in fear of their lives. Mark Antony leads an army that defeats the forces of Brutus, Cassius, and the other plotters. Brutus commits suicide at the end of the battle. Standing over Brutus's dead body, Mark Antony states, "This was the noblest Roman of them all." He explains that the other plotters killed Caesar because of envy of his power, and only the general Brutus acted with "honest thought/And common good to all."

Julius Caesar, like all the plays at the Globe, took place in daylight without the benefit of scenery. All illusions had to be created by the playwright and the actors. Only words and gestures kindled the imagination. When Shakespeare wanted moonlight in *The Merchant of Venice,* he had to evoke each scene through words. For example, Lorenzo tells Jessica:

How sweet the moonlight sleeps upon this bank!
Here will we sit and let the sounds of music
Creep in our ears. Soft stillness and the night
Become the touches of sweet harmony.
Sit, Jessica. Look how the floor of heaven
Is thick inlaid with pantines of bright gold.

—*The Merchant of Venice,* Act V, scene i, 54–59

When Shakespeare wanted a grim night sky, without stars or moon, as in *Macbeth,* his characters created the setting:

BANQUO: How goes the night, boy?
FLEANCE: The moon is down, I have not heard the clock.
BANQUO: And she goes down at twelve.
FLEANCE: I take 't 'tis later, sir.
BANQUO: Hold, take my sword. There's husbandry [economy] in Heaven,
Their candles are all out. . . .

—*Macbeth,* Act II, scene i, 1–5

Shakespeare wrote most of his plays for audiences of a broad social background. A range of people from common laborers to members of the nobility came to the Globe. But most of the audience consisted of middle-class merchants, craftsmen, and their wives.

Audiences of the era were very different from modern audiences. The audience in Shakespeare's time was almost part of the production. Spectators were free to express anger or displeasure at the actions of a villain or to laugh raucously at the antics of a comic hero. In fact, they were expected to. The reaction of the audience was the barometer that told the acting company how well the play was being received. Actors expressed motives, thoughts, and actions with gestures and exclamations that were easily recognized by audiences. Plays were usually based on familiar stories from history, current events, and classical literature. But Shakespeare shaped this material with such genius that he gave it a new sophistication, enlarged its scope, and charged it with greater significance.

Shakespeare's acting career was probably as prolific as his writing career, and acting was much more profitable. He performed on the stage regularly as part of the Lord Chamberlain's Men. In *All's Well That Ends Well*, he played the part of the king. In *Hamlet*, Shakespeare played the ghost. He played the parts of King Henry in *Henry IV*, Suffolk in *Henry VI*, the lord in *The Taming of the Shrew*, and King Philip in *King John*. Because he was an actor as well as a play-

Playing Hamlet is considered by actors to be one of the most difficult theater roles. Sarah Bernhardt (1844–1923), above, *an acclaimed French actor, is dressed for the role.*

wright, Shakespeare had lots of advice for new actors, which he humorously incorporated into the text of his plays. For instance, in *Hamlet*, Act III, scene ii, Shakespeare berates the overacting that he had often witnessed on the stage. He writes:

> Oh, there be players that I
> have seen play, and heard others praise—and that
> highly, not to speak it profanely—that neither hav-
> ing the accent of Christians nor the gait of Christian,
> pagan, nor man, have so strutted and bellowed
> that I have thought some of Nature's journeymen
> had made men, and not made them well, they imi-
> tated humanity so abominably.

> —*Hamlet,* Act III, scene ii, 31–39

In September 1601, records show that Shakespeare returned home to Stratford-upon-Avon to attend his father's funeral. At this time, Shakespeare also began to make real estate investments with some of the money he had earned through his success on the stage. He bought 107 acres in Old Stratford and Bishopton for the sum of 320 pounds (approximately $13,000 in modern money), and by November, he was on his way back to London.

SOME SIXTEENTH-CENTURY INSULTS

hakespeare's plays are filled with insults that were common in the sixteenth century and that can be very comical to a modern reader.

"Show your sheep-biting face, and be hanged in an hour."
—Measure for Measure

"Me think'st thou art a general offence and every man should beat thee."
—All's Well That Ends Well

"There's no more faith in thee than in a stewed prune."
—Henry V

"May the worm of conscience still begnaw thy soul."
—Richard III

Lafeu and Parolles trade insults in Shakespeare's All's Well That Ends Well.

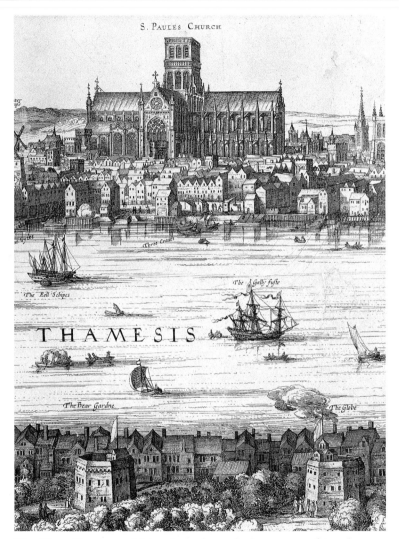

The River Thames, which winds through the center of London, was a bustling trade route and thoroughfare. The Globe Theater is shown in the lower right corner.

Chapter SIX

THE KING'S MEN

*The sixth age shifts
Into the lean and slipper'd Pantaloon,
With spectacles on nose and pouch on side,
His youthful hose, well saved, a world too wide
For his shrunk shank, and his big manly voice,
Turning again toward childish treble, pipes
And whistles in his sound.*

DURING SHAKESPEARE'S TIME, THE CITY OF LONDON was a crammed commercial huddle permeated by the smell of the River Thames. The Thames was everybody's thoroughfare. People normally crossed by boat-taxi, the boatmen calling "Eastward-ho" and "Westward-ho." Gilded barges carried royalty on the waterway. It was not uncommon to see criminals chained to the banks.

London streets were narrow, cobbled, and slippery with the slime of refuse. Houses were crammed together with narrow alleys. Chamber pots holding human waste were emptied out of windows. There was no drainage. But the city had its natural cleansers—the kites, graceful, resourceful birds that made their nests of rags and refuse in the forks of trees. They scavenged, eating anything with relish. And the smells of the countryside floated in—rosy milkmaids in the early morning streets and sellers of newly gathered vegetables.

London was a city of loud noises—the hooves and coach wheels on the cobbles, the yells of traders, the brawling of apprentices. Even normal conversation must have been loud since everybody was, by our standards, tipsy. Nobody drank water, and tea was not yet available. Ale was the standard tipple, and it was strong. Ale for breakfast started the day. Ale for dinner and supper ended the day. The better sort drank wine. It was not a sober city.

In March 1603, Londoners faced a new and difficult situation. Queen Elizabeth became ill, and it became obvious to her advisers that she wouldn't live much longer. Because she didn't have any children, there was no direct heir to the throne. The queen's advisers encouraged her to name her successor before she became too ill. Elizabeth named

James VI of Scotland to become King James I of England shortly before she died on March 24, 1603.

England was just coping with the death of its queen and adjusting to its new ruler when another virulent plague broke out in London in May 1603. The theaters closed on May 26 and remained so for eleven months. By the time the plague epidemic ended, more than thirty thousand people had died. It is not known exactly what thirty-nine-year-old Shakespeare did during the epidemic. He may have returned to Stratford-upon-Avon, or his acting company may have gone on tour in other towns.

The fortune of the Lord Chamberlain's Men soon changed dramatically. The new king appointed the company to be the King's [Men] and Grooms of the Chamber Extraordinary. The players became royal servants, were in frequent demand at court, and were heralded as the most important acting company in the country. They performed more often than any other company in England. Since the players had the protection of the king, they were no longer bothered by religious fanatics and civic authorities bent on closing London's theaters. The King's Men also received the honor of marching with King James I in royal processions, resplendent in scarlet robes that indicated their status as sworn officers of the royal household.

Shakespeare continued to write plays, although his style changed dramatically after writing *Hamlet, All's Well That Ends Well,* and *Measure for Measure.* He began to write with a greater sense of darkness than he had previously displayed. Shakespeare's tragedies *Othello, Macbeth,* and *King Lear* contained a great deal of violence and addressed tragic themes.

The impetus for the creation of *Macbeth* might have stemmed from the assassination attempt on King James I. On November 5, 1605, a man named Guy Fawkes helped lead a group that tried to kill the king. They also tried to blow up both houses of Parliament in protest against the government's hostile attitude toward Roman Catholicism. This much publicized political incident may have inspired Shakespeare to include the killing of a king as a plot in some plays. To this theme, Shakespeare added the elements of the supernatural and witchcraft, common topics during this period of history.

The first scene of *Macbeth* opens on a moor in Scotland. Macbeth and his friend Banquo are returning home when they find three witches stirring a cauldron. As they pass, Banquo notes that the witches appear so strange that they seem not to be alive:

> **BANQUO:** How far is't called to Forres?
> What are these
> So withered, and so wild in their attire,
> That look not like the inhabitants o' the earth
> And yet are on 't? Live you? Or are you aught
> That man may question? You seem to
> understand me. . . .

Guy Fawkes led an attempt on the life of King James I, above, *in November 1605.*

MACBETH: Speak, if you can. What are you?

—*Macbeth,* Act I, scene iii, 39-47

Instead of answering Macbeth's question, the witches begin to predict his future by addressing Macbeth with the various titles he will eventually hold. He thinks they are just senile old women.

> **FIRST WITCH:** All hail, Macbeth! Hail to thee, Thane of Glamis!
> **SECOND WITCH:** All hail, Macbeth, hail to thee, Thane of Cawdor!
> **THIRD WITCH:** All hail, Macbeth, that shalt be King hereafter!

—*Macbeth,* Act I, scene iii, 48–50

The witches appear again in Act IV, scene i, leaning over a cauldron and discussing the fate of Macbeth. Their dialogue is interspersed with a chant:

> FIRST WITCH: Round about the cauldron go.
>   In the poisoned entrails throw.
>   Toad, that under cold stone
>   Days and nights has thirty-one
>   Sweltered venom sleeping got,
>   Boil thou first i' the charmed pot.
> ALL: Double, double toil and trouble,
>   Fire burn and cauldron bubble.
> SECOND WITCH: Fillet of a fenny [swamp] snake,
>   In the cauldron boil and bake.
>   Eye of newt and toe of frog,
>   Wool of bat and tongue of dog,
>   Adder's fork [tongue] and blind worm's sting,
>   Lizard's leg and howlet's [small owl's] wing,
>   For a charm of powerful trouble,
>   Like a Hell broth boil and bubble.
>
> —*Macbeth*, Act IV, scene i, 4–19

The third witch goes on to list the items she is throwing into the boiling pot, items such as scale of dragon and tooth of wolf. The scene with the witches is one of the most famous in Shakespeare's plays. The late sixteenth century was fascinated with the occult and witches in particular.

It was well known at the time that King James I was obsessed with witchcraft. In fact, he had written a very popular book in 1597, entitled *Daemonologie [Demonology]*, in which he instructed readers how to find and kill witches.

In 1605, when Shakespeare wrote *Macbeth*, England was in the throes of a witch craze that had begun earlier in continental Europe. Witches were greatly feared due to old superstitions that were handed down from generation to generation. People hunted down suspected witches. Children turned in their parents, husbands turned in their wives, and neighbors turned in their friends. No one was immune. It is estimated that by the time the witch hunts were over

Macbeth and Banquo encounter the three witches.

WITCHCRAFT

n 1597 King James of Scotland published his famous treatise on witchcraft, called *Daemonologie*. In *Daemonologie*, King James related, allegedly from his own experience, various "facts" about witches, including: witches can cause people to die by burning their image; they can make a person sick by using a wax image and manipulating it in a certain way; and they can cause storms. King James also contended that the devil can trick people by appearing in various disguises, called "familiars," such as dogs, cats, and monkeys. Therefore, any person who kept a pet such as a cat was suspected of being a witch. The crux of the book, however, was his treatise on women as witches. Below is an excerpt on this subject.

> *What can be the cause that there are twenty women given to that craft where there is one man?*

> *Answer: The reason is easy, for as that sex is frailer than man is, so it is easier to be entrapped in these gross snares of the Devil as was ever well proved to be true by the Serpent's deceiving of Eve at the beginning, which makes him the homelier [more familiar] with that sex.*

> *Where the devil finds greatest ignorance and barbarity . . . there assails he grossliest, as I gave you the reason wherefor there was more witches of women kind than men.*

James went on to say that women's vulnerability to the devil made them unfit to rule countries or to have power over men. This philosophy was well received by those who had been displeased with Queen Elizabeth.

This seventeenth-century engraving shows how suspected witches were sometimes tested in water. It was believed that if they were abe to float or swim, they were witches, but if they sank and drowned, they were not.

in the eighteenth century, almost one million people, mostly women, had been unjustly killed in England and Europe, merely on the assumption that they were witches. Shakespeare used this cultural preoccupation with the supernatural in his play to elicit a rich emotional reaction in his audience.

In May 1607, Shakespeare returned home to Stratford-upon-Avon to celebrate the marriage of his daughter Susanna to John Hall, a doctor. Shakespeare stayed at New Place for the remainder of the summer, working on *Antony and Cleopatra* and *Pericles*. Both plays were completed by the time Shakespeare returned to London in October.

The following year, when Susanna gave birth to her daughter, Elizabeth, forty-four-year-old Shakespeare became a grandfather. A few months later, he lost his mother, who died in September 1608.

The following month, the King's Men acquired a private playhouse in London called the Blackfriars Theater. The company used this theater, which was enclosed and easier to reach, as a winter theater. By moving to the Blackfriars, the King's Men dramatically increased profits. However, shortly after the move, another plague broke out in London. The theaters were closed, and Shakespeare retreated to his home in Stratford-upon-Avon, where he continued to write. A new style began to appear in his plays as he shed the dark period of his writing.

He completed *Cymbeline*, a fresh, enchanting play that mixes sadness, humor, near tragedy, fantasy, and poetry. Scholars speculate that he may have been experimenting with a new literary form. Or perhaps, while experiencing the quiet and peace of his new home and gardens, he chose a romantic story that matched the feelings he was experiencing at the time.

Cymbeline, along with *The Winter's Tale* and *The Tempest*, are three plays based on a theme of reconciliation that Shakespeare wrote at the end of his career. The story of Cymbeline is both complicated and far-fetched, even for that era. The story is about a young girl (Imogen) who marries Posthumus for true love. She is harassed by a wicked stepmother (Cloten),

Posthumus, left, *and Imogen,* right, *from Shakespeare's play* Cymbeline

badly treated by her father (Cymbeline, King of Britain), pursued by a hated brute (Iachimo), falsely accused of unfaithfulness, forced to flee disguised as a boy, befriended by mountaineers (who turn out to be her long-lost brothers), and finally returned to her repentant husband. The play is melodramatic and includes battle scenes, a prison scene, ghosts, music, and much moralizing.

In the fall of 1609, Shakespeare returned to London. At this time, he finally allowed his sonnets to be published. Scholars note that Shakespeare had not allowed publication of the sonnets while his mother was living. It is unclear why, although some experts think he feared a negative reaction from her for writing in such a provocative way. Approximately nine months after the death of Shakespeare's mother, publisher

Thomas Thorpe printed a book—*Shake-speares Sonnets: Never before Imprinted*.

During the next few years, Shakespeare continued to perform with the King's Men and to write plays. Shakespeare probably completed *The Winter's Tale* and *The Tempest* in 1610 or 1611. In *The Winter's Tale*, the wrongs committed by one generation are reconciled in the next generation. Leontes, king of Sicilia, falsely accuses his wife, Hermione, of having a love affair with the visiting king of Bohemia, Polixenes. Leontes puts Hermione in prison, where she gives birth to a baby girl, Perdita. Leontes gives orders to have the child killed, but a compassionate soldier secretly takes the child to an island and leaves her there with a family who will raise her. Perdita grows up and falls in love with the prince of Bavaria, Polixenes' son. Polixenes objects to this son marrying a woman he believes to be a commoner, so the couple flees to Sicilia. By the closing scene, Perdita's true identity becomes known, Leontes is filled with remorse, and everyone is finally reconciled.

The Tempest is a romance partly based on several sources, one of which was an actual sea voyage that took place in May 1609. Sir Thomas Gates and his crew set sail on the ship *Sea Adventure* for England's first permanent New World colony, Virginia. The ship was lost at sea and the sailors were shipwrecked on an island near the Bermudas, which was supposedly inhabited by witches and devils. Eventually the crew

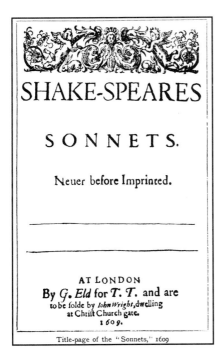

The title page of Shakespeares Sonnets *published in 1609*

SHAKE-SPEARES

S O N N E T S.

Neuer before Imprinted.

AT LONDON
By *G. Eld* for *T. T.* and are
to be folde by *John Wright*, dwelling
at Chrift Church gate.
1 6 0 9.

Title-page of the "Sonnets," 1609

cut down trees and built boats to make its way to Virginia. Stories about their experiences reached England in the early autumn of 1610 and may have inspired Shakespeare.

Written for the court of King James I, *The Tempest* was first performed at a court wedding. The play is a fairy tale with a theme of reconciliation. Old grudges are forgiven, and the characters begin a new life. This play takes place on an enchanted island ruled by Prospero, a magician. He lives there with his daughter, Miranda, and his slave, the monster Caliban. Prospero creates a tempest, or storm, which causes a ship carrying his enemies to crash on the island. Miranda immediately falls in love with Prince Ferdinand, who is also on the ship. Through his magic, Prospero brings the couple together, upsets his enemies' plots, and all ends happily. In this play, Shakespeare blends spectacle, song, and dance with a love story, poetry, and comedy to produce a dramatic fantasy.

Some contemporary scholars believe this play was Shakespeare's farewell to the literary world. They note that in the final scene of the play, the magician Prospero—the main character—closes his books and lays aside his magic cloak. Shakespeare may be telling his audience that, as author and actor, he will soon retire from active life. Toward the end of the fourth act, in one of Shakespeare's most famous speeches, Prospero tells the audience:

> Our revels now are ended. These our actors,
> As I foretold you, were all spirits, and
> Are melted into air, into thin air.
> And, like the baseless fabric [unreal stuff]
>   of this vision,
> The cloud-capped towers, the gorgeous palaces,
> The solemn temples, the great globe itself—
> Yea, all which it inherit—shall dissolve
> And, like this insubstantial pageant faded,
> Leave not a rack [cloud] behind. We are such
>   stuff

As dreams are made on, and our little life
Is rounded with a sleep [life is but a moment of
consciousness in an everlasting sleep].

—*The Tempest,* Act IV, scene i, 148–158

The Globe was constructed of stone, but it had a thatched, or straw, roof, which was highly flammable.

Chapter **SEVEN**

THE FINAL CURTAIN

Last scene of all,
That ends this strange eventful history,
Is second childishness and mere oblivion,
Sans [without] teeth, sans eyes, sans taste,
sans everything.

ON JUNE 29, 1613, THE KING'S MEN WERE performing *Henry VIII* at the Globe Theater. In Act I, scene iv of the play, the actor playing the king enters. That night the King's Men decided to dramatize his entrance by sounding a drum and trumpet and firing a small cannon. This turned out to be an unfortunate decision. The theater's thatched roof caught fire, and in the span of one hour, the Globe burned to the ground.

Shakespeare's plays were very popular, so the Globe had a full house—three thousand playgoers—at the performance that night. No one was seriously hurt, but stories about the fire circulated for months. Many people proudly proclaimed that they had been attending the play when the famous theater burned.

The loss of the theater and its contents, including costumes, set designs, and play scripts, must have been devastating to the King's Men. The end of the Globe signaled the end of Shakespeare's active life in the theater.

At age forty-nine, Shakespeare was ready to retire, and in October 1613, he returned to his house in Stratford-upon-Avon. He made occasional trips to London to take care of business, but for the most part, Shakespeare spent the last years of his life at New Place. Little is known about Shakespeare's life during his retirement years. His peaceful life was disrupted, however, when his daughter Judith decided to accept the marriage proposal of Thomas Quiney in 1616.

Thomas was the son of Richard Quiney, a longtime neighbor and friend of the Shakespeare family. Like his father, Thomas was a tavern keeper. When it was time for him to be married, he chose Judith Shakespeare as his bride. The marriage license for Thomas and Judith was hastily procured, as had been the case with Judith's parents. However, unlike her mother,

Shakespeare eventually moved back to Stratford-upon-Avon and lived in his house, New Place, as illustrated in this engraving.

Judith was not pregnant. There was a different cause for the hasty marriage.

Thomas Quiney had had an affair with another woman while he was courting Judith, and this woman had given birth to a child. Thomas knew this information was about to be made public and that Judith would not marry him if she discovered the truth. Quiney obtained a license to marry Judith on February 10, 1616, before she found out the real state of affairs. Two months later, the story about Thomas's former mistress became known, causing grave embarrassment to the family and to the well-known William Shakespeare in particular.

Most people considered Thomas Quiney to be a rogue and a scoundrel. He had entered marriage under false pretenses. In addition, he had been accused of drunkenness and of cursing his patrons on several occasions.

In January 1616, Shakespeare summoned lawyer Francis Collins to draw up the first draft of his last will and testament. A second version was drafted in March.

The will lists the properties and money to be divided between Shakespeare's two daughters. Through the will, Shakespeare wanted to safeguard Judith's interests and make her as independent as possible from a husband he did not trust.

According to the terms of the will, Judith was to receive one hundred pounds plus another fifty pounds if she gave up her claim to Chapel Lane cottage. She would receive an additional one hundred and fifty pounds after three years if she or any children she might have were still living. As long as she remained married, however, she would be paid only a small part of the money each year. Shakespeare's will stated specifically that Quiney was not to touch any of this money.

Shakespeare's other daughter, Susanna, was to receive Shakespeare's personal property, which included New Place, three additional houses, and some land.

Susanna was to inherit Shakespeare's investments outside Stratford-upon-Avon, including his shares in the
Globe and Blackfriars Theaters and his property in
the Blackfriars section of London.

He willed all his clothes and twenty pounds to his sister, Joan, and willed that she be permitted to live the
rest of her days in her Henley Street house. To his wife,
Anne, he bequeathed his bed—not his best bed, but his
second best bed. Shakespeare's wife, by law, should
have received one-third of her husband's estate. It is
not possible to know what Shakespeare's intent was. It
may have been a cold, callous bequest, or it may have
been a loving one. The second best bed was probably
the marriage bed, the best bed being reserved for the
many guests who stayed at New Place. But no one
knows for sure. Shakespeare left his sword to Thomas
Combe, the nephew and heir of his friend John Combe,
who had died two years earlier. Shakespeare left "the
poore of Stratford" ten pounds, a large sum of money
in those days. He named several close friends in his
will, among them John Heminge, Richard Burbage,
and Henry Condell. He declared that twenty-six
shillings and eight pence were to be given to each of
the three men to buy memorial rings.

On April 23, 1616, after a sudden fever, William
Shakespeare died on what is thought to have been his
fifty-second birthday. The exact nature of his illness is
unknown, but it is recorded that he had been in bad
health for a few weeks. John Ward, the vicar of

The epitaph on Shakespeare's gravestone reads: Good friend for Jesus Sake Forbeare,/To Digg the dust enclosed heare:/Blesse be [the] man [who] spares thes stones,/and curst be he [who] moves my bones.

Stratford-upon-Avon, wrote in his diary that Shakespeare died after a visit with friends: "Shakespear, Drayton and Ben Jhonson [a famous writer of the era] had a merry meeting and it seems drank too hard for it seems Shakespear died of a feavour thee [fever he] contracted." Two days later, Shakespeare was buried in Holy Trinity Church. It is said that his grave was dug seventeen feet deep to insure that no one would dig up the popular playwright's bones.

Shakespeare had an elaborate funeral and was buried in the church proper rather than in the churchyard. As a monument in his honor, a bust of Shakespeare stands in Holy Trinity Church. Scholars consider the bust one of only two authentic likenesses of Shakespeare.

No blood descendents of Shakespeare lived beyond the seventeenth century. His daughter Susanna gave birth to three children, all of whom died without offspring. Judith also had three children who died

This bust of Shakespeare stands in Holy Trinity Church in Stratford-upon-Avon. It is considered one of only two authentic representations of Shakespeare.

young, the last two in 1639. Shakespeare's bloodline died out with the death of the last of his grandchildren in 1674.

No original manuscripts of Shakespeare's plays exist. Modern versions are based on early published texts called quartos and folios. (A quarto is a small volume containing a single Shakespeare play. A folio contains a collection of his plays.) In 1623, seven years after Shakespeare died and the same year that Anne Shakespeare died, the *First Folio* was printed. The folio, which contained thirty-six of Shakespeare's plays, was a tremendous undertaking. The work was a genuine tribute of affection on the part of Isaac Jaggard, a printer, and Edward Blount, a bookseller. Shakespeare's fellow actors John Heminge and Henry Condell edited the collection. The plays are arranged by genre: histories, comedies, and tragedies.

The most impressive tribute in the folio is an ode written by Shakespeare's friend Ben Jonson. It is known for these famous lines:

> He was not of an age, but for all time!
> And all the Muses still were in their prime
> When like Apollo he came forth to warm
> Our ears, or like a Mercury to charm.
> Nature herself was proud of his designs,
> And joyed to wear the dressing of his lines,
> Which were so richly spun, and woven so fit,
> As, since, she will vouchsafe no other Wit.

The merry Greek, tart Aristophanes,
Neat Terence, witty Plautus, now not please;
But antiquated and deserted lie
As they were not of Nature's family.
Yet must I not give Nature all; thy Art,
My gentle Shakespeare, must enjoy a part.
For though the poet's matter Nature be,
His Art doth give the fashion. And that he
Who casts to write a living line must sweat,
(Such as thine are) and strike the second heat
Upon the Muses' anvil: turn the same,
And himself with it, that he thinks to frame;
Or for the laurel, he may gain a scorn;
For a good poet's made, as well as born.
And such wert thou!

The tributes given to William Shakespeare have never been given to any other poet or playwright. In fact, the world has never stopped paying homage to William Shakespeare.

Chart of English Monarchs from Henry VII to James I

Henry VII
Reigned from 1485 to 1509

Henry VIII
Son of Henry VII and Elizabeth of York
Reigned from 1509 to 1547

Edward VI
Son of Henry VIII and Jane Seymour
Reigned from 1547 to 1553

Mary I
Daughter of Henry VIII and Catherine of Aragon
Reigned from 1553 to 1558

Elizabeth I
Daughter of Henry VIII and Anne Boleyn
Reigned from 1558 to 1603

James I
Son of Mary, Queen of Scots and Henry Stuart (also
known as Lord Darnley)
Reigned from 1603 to 1625

GENEALOGY OF THE SHAKESPEARE FAMILY

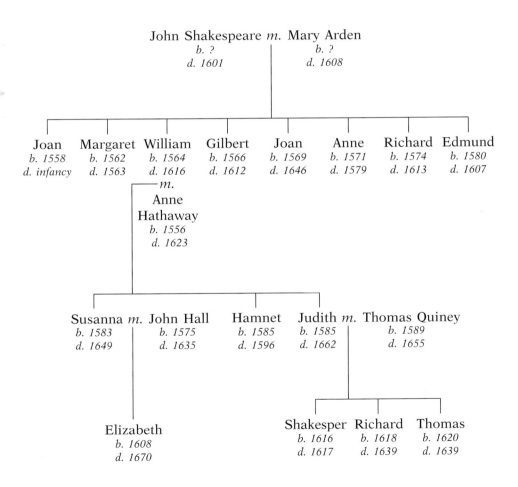

John Shakespeare *m.* Mary Arden
b. ?   *b. ?*
d. 1601   *d. 1608*

Joan
b. 1558
d. infancy

Margaret
b. 1562
d. 1563

William
b. 1564
d. 1616
m.
Anne
Hathaway
b. 1556
d. 1623

Gilbert
b. 1566
d. 1612

Joan
b. 1569
d. 1646

Anne
b. 1571
d. 1579

Richard
b. 1574
d. 1613

Edmund
b. 1580
d. 1607

Susanna *m.* John Hall
b. 1583   *b. 1575*
d. 1649   *d. 1635*

Hamnet
b. 1585
d. 1596

Judith *m.* Thomas Quiney
b. 1585   *b. 1589*
d. 1662   *d. 1655*

Elizabeth
b. 1608
d. 1670

Shakesper
b. 1616
d. 1617

Richard
b. 1618
d. 1639

Thomas
b. 1620
d. 1639

THE LIFE OF SHAKESPEARE

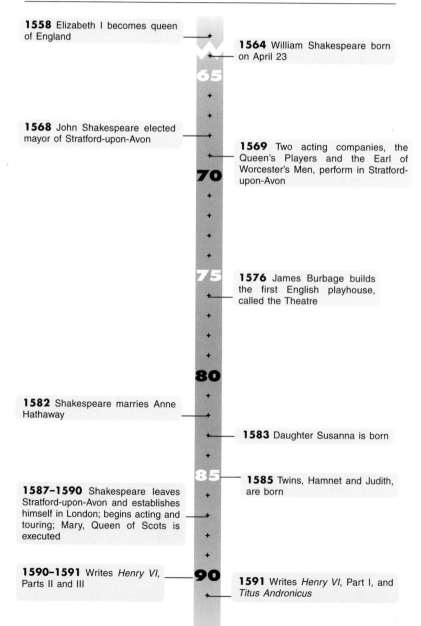

1558 Elizabeth I becomes queen of England

1564 William Shakespeare born on April 23

1568 John Shakespeare elected mayor of Stratford-upon-Avon

1569 Two acting companies, the Queen's Players and the Earl of Worcester's Men, perform in Stratford-upon-Avon

1576 James Burbage builds the first English playhouse, called the Theatre

1582 Shakespeare marries Anne Hathaway

1583 Daughter Susanna is born

1585 Twins, Hamnet and Judith, are born

1587–1590 Shakespeare leaves Stratford-upon-Avon and establishes himself in London; begins acting and touring; Mary, Queen of Scots is executed

1590–1591 Writes *Henry VI*, Parts II and III

1591 Writes *Henry VI*, Part I, and *Titus Andronicus*

1592–1593 Plague strikes; Shakespeare begins writing his sonnets; writes *The Comedy of Errors* and *The Taming of the Shrew*; Robert Greene's attack is published

1593 Shakespeare dedicates *Venus and Lucrece* to Henry Wriothesley, third earl of Southhampton; completes *The Two Gentlemen of Verona*, *Love's Labor's Lost*, and *Richard III*

1594 The Lord Chamberlain's Men is formed; *The Rape of Lucrece* is published

1594–1596 Shakespeare gains more fame and recognition as the leading poet and playwright in London; son Hamnet dies; Shakespeare completes *A Midsummer Night's Dream*, *Romeo and Juliet*, *Richard II*, and *The Merchant of Venice*

1597 Shakespeare buys New Place; writes *Henry IV*, Parts I and II

1598 Writes *As You Like It* and *Much Ado about Nothing*

1599 The Globe Theater opens; Shakespeare completes *The Merry Wives of Windsor*, *Henry V*, and *Julius Caesar*

1601 John Shakespeare dies

1603 Elizabeth I dies; King James I is crowned king of England; the Lord Chamberlain's Men become the King's Men

1604 Writes *Measure for Measure* and *Othello*

1605 Writes *King Lear;* invests in properties in Stratford-upon-Avon

1607 Susanna marries Dr. John Hall; Shakespeare writes *Antony and Cleopatra*

1608 Plague strikes; Shakespeare's mother dies; King's Men acquire Blackfriars Theater; granddaughter Elizabeth Hall is born; Shakespeare writes *Coriolanus*

1609 Completes *Pericles*, *Macbeth*, and *Timon of Athens*; publication of the sonnets

1610 Writes *Cymbeline*

1611 Writes *The Winter's Tale* and *Henry VIII*

1612 Writes *The Tempest*

1613 Shakespeare retires from London life and returns to Stratford-upon-Avon; the Globe burns down; Richard Shakespeare dies

1616 Judith Shakespeare marries Thomas Quiney; Shakespeare dies on April 23

1623 Anne Hathaway Shakespeare dies; *First Folio* is published

THE COMPLETE WORKS OF WILLIAM SHAKESPEARE

THE PLAYS

All's Well That Ends Well
Antony and Cleopatra
As You Like It
The Comedy of Errors
Coriolanus
Cymbeline
Hamlet
Henry IV, Parts I and II
Henry V
Henry VI, Parts I, II, and III
Henry VIII
Julius Caesar
King John
King Lear
Love's Labor's Lost
Macbeth
Measure for Measure
The Merchant of Venice
The Merry Wives of Windsor
A Midsummer Night's Dream
Much Ado about Nothing
Othello

Pericles
Richard II
Richard III
Romeo and Juliet
The Taming of the Shrew
The Tempest
Timon of Athens
Titus Andronicus
Troilus and Cressida
Twelfth Night
The Two Gentlemen of Verona
The Winter's Tale

THE POEMS

A Lover's Complaint
The Passionate Pilgrim
The Phoenix and the Turtle
The Rape of Lucrece
Sonnets
Venus and Adonis

SOURCES

17 Marchette Chute, *Shakespeare of London* (New York: E. P. Dutton & Co. Inc., 1949), 3.

17 Ibid., 4.

27 Edgar I. Fripp, *Master Richard Quyny* (London: Oxford University Press, 1974), n.p.

32 Russell Fraser, *Young Shakespeare* (New York: Columbia University Press, 1988), 113.

32 Park Honan, *Shakespeare: A Life* (New York: Oxford University Press, 2000), 84.

36 P. J. P. Goldberg, *Women in England c. 1275-1525* (Manchester and New York: Manchester University Press, 1995), 167–168.

37 Honan, 83.

44 Terry A. Gray, *1592 Upstart Crow,* April 24, 1998, <http://daphne.palomar.edu/shakespeare/timeline/crow.htm> (n.d.).

80 Selma Williams and Pamela Williams Adelman, *Riding the Nightmare: Women and Witchcraft from the Old World to Colonial Salem* (New York: Harper Perennial, 1978), 255.

94 Edmund K. Chambers, *William Shakespeare: A Study of the Facts and Problems* (Oxford: Clarendon Press, 1930), 145.

96–97 *The Complete Pelican Shakespeare*, ed. Alfred Harbage (New York: Penguin Books, 1969), n.p.

BIBLIOGRAPHY

Adams, John Cranford. *The Globe Playhouse: Its Design and Equipment*. Cambridge: Harvard University Press, 1942.

Alexander, Peter. *Shakespeare's Life and Art*. London: James Nisbet and Company, Ltd., 1939.

Anspacher, Louis K. *Shakespeare as Poet and Lover and the Enigma of the Sonnets*. Brooklyn, New York: Haskell House Publishers, Ltd., 1973.

Ashby, Ruth. *Elizabethan England*. New York: Benchmark Books, 1999.

Asimov, Isaac. *Asimov's Guide to Shakespeare*. New York: Wings Books, 1970.

Barrett, W. P. *Present Remedies Against the Plague*. London: Shakespeare Association Facsimiles, no. 7, 1933.

Bentley, Nicholas. *Tales from Shakespeare*. New York: Simon & Schuster, 1972.

Brode, Douglas. *Shakespeare in the Movies*. New York: Oxford University Press, 2000.

Brooks, Alden. *William Shakespeare and the Dyer's Hand*. New York: Charles Scribner's Sons, 1943.

Brown, Ivor. *Shakespeare: A Biography and An Interpretation*. New York: Doubleday and Company, Inc., 1949.

Burgess, Anthony. *Shakespeare*. Chicago: Ivan R. Dee, Inc., 1970.

Chambers, Edmund K. *The Elizabethan Stage*. Oxford: Clarendon Press, 1923.

_____. *William Shakespeare: A Study of the Facts and Problems*. Oxford: Clarendon Press, 1930.

Chaucer, Geoffrey. *The Canterbury Tales*. From the text of W. W. Skeat, London: Oxford University Press, 1906.

Chute, Marchette. *Shakespeare of London*. New York: E. P. Dutton & Co. Inc., 1949.

De Chambrun, Clara Longworth. *Shakespeare Rediscovered*. New York: Charles Scribner's Sons, 1938.

Eccles, Mark. *Shakespeare in Warwickshire*. Madison,Wisconsin: University of Wisconsin Press, 1961.

Emerson, Kathy Lynn. *The Writer's Guide to Everyday Life in*

Renaissance England from 1485-1649. Cincinnati, Ohio: The Writer's Digest Books, 1996.

Fraser, Russell. *Young Shakespeare.* New York: Columbia University Press, 1988.

Fripp, Edgar I. *Shakespeare's Stratford.* London: Oxford University Press, 1928.

_____. *Shakespeare Studies.* London: Oxford University Press, 1930.

Goldberg, P. J. P. *Women in England c. 1275–1525.* Manchester and New York: Manchester University Press, 1995.

Gray, Terry A. *1592 Upstart Crow.* April 24, 1998. <http://daphne.palomar.edu/shakespeare/timeline/crow.htm> (n.d.).

Guazzo, Francesco Maria. *Compendium Maleficarum.* New York: Dover Publications, Inc., 1988.

Haigh, Christopher. *Elizabeth I.* New York: Addison-Wesley, Inc., 1998.

Harrison, G. B. *Shakespeare: The Complete Works.* New York: Harcourt, Brace and World, Inc., 1968.

Honan, Park. *Shakespeare: A Life.* New York: Oxford University Press, 2000.

Hugo, Victor. *William Shakespeare.* Boston: Dana Estes and Co., 1864.

Kay, Dennis. *Shakespeare: His Life, Work, and Era.* New York: William Morrow and Company, Inc., 1992.

Levi, Peter. *The Life and Times of William Shakespeare.* New York: Henry Holt & Company, 1988.

Lewis, B. Roland. *The Shakespeare Documents.* Stanford, California: Stanford University Press, 1940.

Macardle, Dorothy. *Shakespeare: Man and Boy.* London: Faber and Faber, 1961.

Macdonald, Ronald R. *William Shakespeare: The Comedies.* New York: Twayne Publishers, 1992.

Nagler, A. M. *Shakespeare's Stage.* New Haven: Yale University Press, 1958.

Quennell, Peter. *Shakespeare.* New York: The World Publishing Company, 1963.

Reese, M. M. *Shakespeare: His World and His Work.* New York: St. Martin's Press, 1980.

Rolfe, William J. *Shakespeare the Boy.* 1896. Reprint, New York: Frederick Ungar Publishing Co., 1965.

Rowse, A. L. *Sex and Society in Shakespeare's Age: Simon Forman the Astrologer.* New York: Oxford University Press, 1974.

_____. *Shakespeare, the Elizabethan.* New York: G. P. Putnam Sons, 1977.

_____. *Shakespeare the Man.* New York: Harper and Row Publishers, 1973.

_____. *William Shakespeare.* New York: Harper and Row Publishers, 1963.

Russell, Jeffrey B. *A History of Witchcraft.* London: Thames and Hudson, Ltd., 1980.

Sams, Eric. *The Real Shakespeare.* New Haven: Yale University Press, 1995.

Shellard, Dominic. *William Shakespeare.* Oxford: Oxford University Press, 1998.

Trewin, J. C. *Shakespeare on the English Stage: 1900–1964.* London: Barrie and Rockliff, 1964.

Williams, Selma, and Pamela Williams Adelman. *Riding the Nightmare: Women and Witchcraft from the Old World to Colonial Salem.* New York: Harper Perennial, 1978.

Wright, Louis B. *Middle-Class Culture in Elizabethan England.* Chapel Hill: The University of North Carolina Press, 1935.

FOR FURTHER READING

Aagesen, Colleen. *Shakespeare for Kids: His Life and Times*. Chicago: Chicago Review Press, 1999.

Aliki. *William Shakespeare and the Globe*. New York: Harper Collins Publishers, 1999.

Ashby, Ruth. *Elizabeth's England*. New York: Benchmark Books, 1999.

Birch, Beverly. *Shakespeare Stories: Histories*. New York: P. Bedrick Books, 1988.

Garfield, Leon. *Shakespeare's Stories*. New York: Schocken Books, 1985.

Green, Robert. *Queen Elizabeth I*. New York: Franklin Watts, Inc., 1997.

Macbeth. Retold by Bruce Coville. New York: Dial Books, 1997.

Middleton, Hayden. *William Shakespeare: The Master Playwright*. New York: Oxford University Press, 1998.

Nikola-Lisa, W. *Till Year's Good End: A Calendar of Medieval Labours*. New York: Atheneum, 1997.

O'Brien, Patrick. *The Making of a Knight: How Sir James Earned His Armor.* Watertown, Massachusetts: Charlesbridge, 1998.

Pollinger, Gina. *Macbeth.* Retold by Bruce Coville. New York: Dial Books, 1997.

_____. *Romeo and Juliet.* Retold by Billy Aronson. New York: Harper Paperbacks, 1996.

_____. *Something Rich and Strange: A Treasury of Shakespeare's Verse.* New York: Kingfisher, 1995.

_____. *The Tempest.* Retold by Ann Keay. New York: Philomel Books, 1996.

Stanley, Diane. *Good Queen Bess.* New York: Four Winds Press, 1990.

Thrasher, Thomas. *William Shakespeare.* San Diego: Lucent Press, 1999.

Turk, Ruth. *The Play's the Thing: A Story about William Shakespeare.* Minneapolis: Carolrhoda Books, 1998.

Williams, Marcia. *Tales from Shakespeare.* Cambridge, Massachusetts.: Candlewick Press, 1998.

INDEX

OTHER TITLES FROM LERNER AND A&E®:

Arthur Ashe
The Beatles
Benjamin Franklin
Bill Gates
Bruce Lee
Carl Sagan
Chief Crazy Horse
Christopher Reeve
Edgar Allan Poe
Eleanor Roosevelt
George W. Bush
George Lucas
Gloria Estefan
Jack London
Jacques Cousteau
Jane Austen
Jesse Owens
Jesse Ventura
Jimi Hendrix
John Glenn
Latin Sensations

Legends of Dracula
Legends of Santa Claus
Louisa May Alcott
Madeleine Albright
Malcolm X
Mark Twain
Maya Angelou
Mohandas Gandhi
Mother Teresa
Nelson Mandela
Oprah Winfrey
Princess Diana
Queen Cleopatra
Queen Latifah
Rosie O'Donnell
Saint Joan of Arc
Thurgood Marshall
Wilma Rudolph
Women in Space
Women of the Wild West

ABOUT THE AUTHOR

Carol Dommermuth-Costa has worked in the classroom as a teacher and in publishing as an editor. She teaches creative writing for adults. Ms. Dommermuth-Costa has also written *Nikola Tesla: A Spark of Genius, Agatha Christie: Writer of Mystery, Emily Dickinson: Singular Poet,* and *Indira Gandhi: Daughter of India,* and an upcoming biography of Woodrow Wilson. She lives in Mamaroneck, New York, with her two adult children.